IMAGES
of America

WICHITA
1930–2000

Dr. Edward Tihen was a passionate collector and researcher as well as a physician. A number of images, including some in this book, come from his collection. Equally significant, he devoted himself to creating an index to *The Wichita Eagle*. A version is available online at specialcollections. wichita.edu. (Courtesy Wichita-Sedgwick County Historical Museum.)

ON THE COVER: These people are waiting to get inside the Crest Theater to see Elvis Presley's *Loving You* around 1957. The Crest Theater closed in 1989 and was demolished in 1997. (Courtesy Wichita-Sedgwick County Historical Museum.)

IMAGES
of America

WICHITA
1930–2000

Jay M. Price and Keith Wondra

ARCADIA
PUBLISHING

Published by Arcadia Publishing
Charleston, South Carolina

Library of Congress Control Number: 2012949540

For all general information, please contact Arcadia Publishing:
Telephone 843-853-2070
Fax 843-853-0044
E-mail sales@arcadiapublishing.com
For customer service and orders:
Toll-Free 1-888-313-2665

Visit us on the Internet at www.arcadiapublishing.com

H. Craig Miner, professor of History at Wichita State University, was one of the most respected and prolific authors who wrote about Kansas and Wichita. His *Wichita: The Magic City* is still the premier text about the community. (Courtesy Jay M. Price.)

CONTENTS

ACKNOWLEDGMENTS

Writing the history of a city is a daunting, humbling task. The buildings, economic data, and demographics are intertwined with countless individual stories, fateful decisions, and chance encounters. Each neighborhood, thoroughfare, family, business, and institution has a deep, rich history, every one worthy of its own book. Therefore, a community's story over several decades is inherently a sampling of what took place rather than a comprehensive, exhaustive study.

The Wichita-Sedgwick County Historical Museum sponsored the writing of this book, partly with the goal of highlighting the museum's photograph and artifact collections. Unless otherwise noted, all photographs presented here are from the museum. The authors, therefore, are grateful to director Eric Cale for making this project possible. Particular thanks goes to Jami Frazier Tracy, who brought out literally thousands of images to consider and answered endless questions about the materials. As extensive as the museum's collection is, however, other institutions, businesses, and persons provided photographs and information. Thanks also need to go to Special Collections and University Archives, Wichita State University Libraries (including Dr. Lorraine Madway and Mary Nelson); Wichita Public Library (including Michelle Enke); Sedgwick County Records Management (including Doug King, Melissa Thompson and Austin Rhodes); McCormick School Museum (including Paul Oberg); Kansas Aviation Museum (including Lon Smith and Dave Moreno); Koch Industries; Augusta Historical Museum; Independent School (including Karen Norton); Wichita Asian Association; Wichita Park Department (including Doug Kupper and Christina Butler); Wichita Police Department (including Cpt. Darrell Attebury); Mid-America All-Indian Center; Kansas African American Museum; Newsbank Readex; Old Cowtown Museum; Botanica, The Wichita Gardens (including Marty Miller); *The Wichita Eagle* (including Brian Corn and Beccy Tanner); National Baseball Congress (including Casey Walkup); Orpheum Theatre (including Jennifer Wright); Catholic Diocese of Wichita; Interfaith Ministries; Wichita Community Theater; KU Medical Center; KPTS; KMUW; Riordan Clinic; Kings-X; Nu Way; Old Mill Tasty Shop; Town and Country; Spirit AeroSystems; 22nd Air Refueling Wing; Jedd Beaudoin; Robert Branaman; Beverly Calvert; James Crawford; Myra Devlin; Janiece Baum Dixon; Wayne Gottstine; Richard Harris; Mike Harvey; Hephner family; Grant Hewitt; Jack Kellogg; George Laughead; Jim Mason; MyPictureman; Dave Rodriquez; Thane Rogers; Lisa Rundstrom; Linda and Melvin Saffier; Mark Shock; David Simmonds; Dudley Toevs; Joachim Walther family, and Nestor Weigand. Thanks also go to the numerous photographers and their families, both named and unnamed, that produced the images that appear in this book

INTRODUCTION

Wichita, Kansas, is a complicated place. With strong ties to military and general aviation, it has an established history as a company town. For generations, local life has been intertwined with the fortunes and challenges of Boeing, Beechcraft, Cessna, and later, Learjet. Shift changes—not the classic 9-to-5 office hours—have often governed the pulse of daily events. Workers knew that if one company laid off employees, they could "cross Oliver" to a neighboring firm that was hiring. Similar stories took place among those who built and worked for Coleman, Koch, Love Box, Derby Oil, the Livestock Exchange, Cudahy, or the mills and elevators along the city's northern edge. In many ways, Wichita has been a classic, blue-collar, Midwest industrial city.

Wichita has been a crossroads of ideas and issues. It is where the North, the South, the East the West, the Midwest, and the Southwest all meet with the values and ideals of each of those regions coming together and sometimes clashing. Wichita has been at the forefront of a national discussion about race, segregation, and integration, a center for civil rights activism that also gave rise to several African American business and political figures. In 1966, Allen Ginsberg wrote his "Wichita Vortex Sutra" that contrasted the turbulence of the Vietnam era with the placidness of conservative Midwestern values, a fitting vignette for a city that helped shape both the Beat Movement and modern conservatism.

In many instances, Wichita has been a mosaic of varied areas and neighborhoods as much as a single place. Wichitans often speak of their city through its divisions. They talk about "the East Side" versus "the West Side," with those from the south side and communities such as Derby, Andover, Goddard, Maize, and Bel Aire adding to the complexity. To Wichitans, high school ties can convey a wealth of class, ethnic, racial, and cultural nuances that can define individuals' lives. Colleges such as Wichita State University, Friends University, and Newman University are community institutions, yet are distinct anchors for their respective sections of the city.

In other ways, however, Wichita functions akin to a large small town with common traditions and institutions evoking nostalgic memories. Yet, Wichitans, who sometimes refer to their city with the affectionate nickname of "Doo-Dah," also share many common traditions and institutions. For decades, downtown was the place everyone went, regardless of their neighborhood. Several generations remembered "dragging Douglas" as a rite of passage; their children and grandchildren may speak of meeting friends at Old Town in similar terms in the years to come. Whether a resident of Eastborough or Westlink, Vickridge or Oaklawn, all could share beloved television figures and programs, attend Riverfest, or have fun at Joyland.

Now well into the 21st century, Wichita is finding itself once again in transition. Aviation remains but defined through a new set of companies, including Airbus, Bombardier, and Spirit. Education and health care have become ever greater elements in the local economy. Older industries such as oil refining and meatpacking are largely gone, but new technologies and wind power are gaining visibility. The executives' families that formed the bedrock of the local elite have relocated to new corporate headquarters elsewhere or followed children and grandchildren to other cities. Meanwhile, a new generation of residents—with roots in Chicago, Saigon/Ho Chi Minh City, and Juarez—is just starting to make itself heard. When a future scholar writes the sequel to this work, Wichita will likely be a very different yet no less intriguing city.

In late 1926, Travel Air purchased six acres of land on East Central Avenue that gained the moniker "Travel Air City." Factory E, its saw-tooth roofline quite evident in this sketch, was completed in 1929. Travel Air eventually became part of a larger conglomerate that included Curtiss-Wright. A few years later, the company closed this plant. In 1934, however, Walter Beech reopened the facility under the banner of his own company, Beechcraft.

One

FROM DEPRESSION TO WAR

In the 1930s, as the Depression continued and dust from western Kansas drifted in the air, Wichita worked to keep its aviation industry alive. New Deal efforts brought some relief, even transforming the physical landscape of the city. The arrival of World War II brought a new level of prosperity as the city transitioned almost overnight into a 24-hour-a-day community. By 1943, Wichita's population stood at nearly 190,000—almost double what it had been during much of the 1930s. Those who sought work during the Great Depression struggled to find housing during the war years. One result was the creation of new neighborhoods and communities such as Planeview, Hilltop Manor, and Beechwood. Demand for military aircraft ended even more suddenly than it began. In late 1945, companies such as Boeing simply stopped production, with some aircraft going directly from assembly line to scrap heap. There was fear that Wichita might follow suit.

J.P. Weigand said: "I am for Wichita. Wichita is the Indianapolis of the Southwest. The greatest commercial and financial center of its size in the world, 15 lines of railroad radiate into a territory with 700,000 people within 100 miles of Wichita; wherein the future will live 1,000,000 people, with Wichita as their metro point . . . Watch us grow."

The Wichita Eagle boasted in 1930 that "the City of Wichita points with pride to the new Allis, a friendly hotel." Kansas City, Missouri, hotel magnate Barney L. Allis commissioned the architectural firm of Schmidt, Boucher, and Overend to design the 17-story tower. George H. Siedhoff, a prominent Wichita builder, oversaw the construction of what was Kansas's tallest structure.

With the completion of the federal building and post office in 1932, the old post office at William and Market was no longer needed and was eventually demolished down to its foundation to become a parking lot.

Until the 1950s, Central Avenue was the main artery east out of Wichita. Along its route stood businesses such as Gilbert Johnson's store, above, complete with Art Deco designs executed in a form of concrete decoration known as Carthalite. Continuing east, a driver would have left College Hill and driven through farmland, seeing the radio tower for KFH just before reaching the Beechcraft plant located in the old Travel Air facility.

In 1930, J. Arch Butts moved his Packard dealership from North Broadway Street to Douglas Avenue, "Wichita's Auto Row." By the time of this image, it was home to the Butts Auto Company. It later served as home to Hobbs Chevrolet.

Leo L. McKenzie was the owner of McKenzie Body Works at 117 West First Street. Although his main business involved automotive repair, McKenzie also created the "Midget Auto," a small vehicle intended for children. Here, two McKenzie Midgets appear in a parade.

Claude Neon Federal Sign Company at Douglas Avenue and New York Street opened in 1929, later renamed Claude Federal Sign and Awning. Among the company's projects were the lettering that topped the Allis Hotel, as well as the marquees for the Miller and Orpheum Theatres in Wichita as well as the Anthony Theater and Hutchinson's Fox Theatre.

"We only went to the [Innes Department Store] Tea Room about once a month as it was more formal; I wore a hat and gloves then, and it was a special treat. Actually, hats were very popular and there was a sizeable millinery department in Innes. I don't have a clue now on how expensive the Tea Room food was but at the time it seemed expensive!" said Beverly Klicker Calvert.

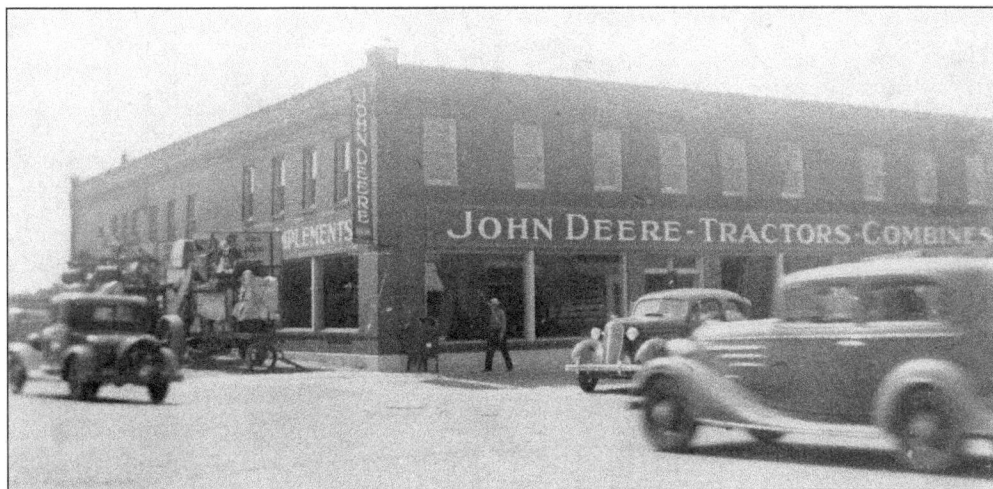

Located south of downtown between Douglas Avenue and Lewis Street, the dealers of "Tractor Row" specialized in farm implements and equipment. A 1925 article in *The Wichita Eagle* said, "During the buying season, which extends from spring until fall, the thoroughfare is the busiest spot in Wichita," a feature that continued until urban renewal efforts in the 1960s. A string of grain elevators and flour mills extended north of downtown along the main railroad tracks. Among them was the facility of Kansas Milling, seen below, located at 715 East Thirteenth Street.

Beechcraft looked to the luxury aviation market for its survival. Its first major venture was the Model 17 or Staggerwing, called so because the upper wing of this biplane was staggered back on the aircraft with the lower one more to the fore. These Staggerwings are under construction in the Beech plant in the old Travel Air facility. Below is Cessna's airplane, the C-38, or Airmaster. Dwayne Wallace is at the helm of this Airmaster; he took over the leadership of Cessna after his uncle's retirement. (Both, courtesy Kansas Aviation Museum.)

Wichita's initial air terminal, seen above, opened in 1929 and was a major stop in early transcontinental airmail routes. A few years later, on March 31, 1935, fifteen thousand people braved heavy mist and a near-freezing temperature to attend the dedication ceremony of a large, new administration building. In the years that followed, it was such a popular hangout, especially to see visiting celebrities, that local businessman Walter Vincent dubbed the new building "a country club without any dues." During World War II, the original 1929 terminal building burned, while the newer 1930s one gained two additional wings and a modern control tower. (Both, courtesy Kansas Aviation Museum.)

Cattle and meat have been central to Wichita's story since the 1870s. By the 1930s, the area northeast of Twenty-first and Broadway Streets included the packing plants of Cudahy, whose workers are seen here, and Dold. Immediately to the east, where Chisholm Creek and Twenty-first Street intersected, stood the Wichita Live Stock Exchange.

Just to the east of the stockyards stood the Derby Oil Company's Refinery along Twenty-first Street. Founded in 1920, the company had, in just a few years, expanded to include a series of local filling stations and a refinery, the loading rack of which is seen here. The refinery's operations continued until 1993.

Oilman Archibald Derby is seated on
the left in the great room of his residence
at 320 North Belmont. Robert Clapp,
son of park advocate L.W. Clapp, built
the Tudor Revival structure in 1926.
Derby and his wife Ida purchased the
home in 1944. Wichita icon Olive White
Garvey later lived at this address.

Another of Wichita's major oil figures,
John A. "Jack" Vickers, escorts his
daughter Helen at her wedding to
Preston Clark in September 1940.
Two months later, illness claimed Jack
Vickers's life. Vickers began in the Butler
County oil fields, including a refinery
at Potwin. His most famous endeavor,
however, may have been his expansive
estate, Vickridge, located on Central
Avenue, then outside the city limits.

Marcellus Murdock was the son of *The Wichita Eagle* founder Marshall Murdock Beginning his 60-year career with *The Wichita Eagle* in 1902, Murdock later launched an evening edition of it to compete with its longtime rival, the *Wichita Beacon*. (Courtesy Kansas Aviation Museum.)

From left to right, brothers Max, John, and Louis Levand (with the pressroom manager on the far right) joined forces in 1928 to take on the *Wichita Beacon*. Max was general manager with John in charge of circulation and Louis as publisher. The *Beacon* persisted under the Levands' guidance until 1960 when *The Wichita Eagle* acquired it. (Courtesy Melvin and Linda Saffier.)

The varied programs of the New Deal transformed the landscape of Wichita. In one of the earliest public works programs, the Civil Works Administration (CWA) filled in the channel separating Ackerman Island from the west bank of the Arkansas River. By the time of this photograph, the "island" was no more. Public works programs improved wages and opportunities but did not end labor troubles, as seen in the labor strike below. In some cases, labor unrest took place because local employers could not match the relatively decent wages of New Deal work.

One of the main events of the Kansas Diamond Jubilee of 1936 was an exposition in Wichita. During the event at Lawrence Stadium, Pres. Franklin Delano Roosevelt said, "By and large, we are coming through a great national crisis with flying colors. We have not lost our self-respect."

This parade of cars down Douglas Avenue dates from the time of Kansas's 75th anniversary celebrations. Whether the motorcade contains President Roosevelt or another dignitary is unknown.

In 1935, the United States Veterans Administration opened a medical facility on the eastern edge of town, at Kellogg Avenue and Bleckley Drive. Although the main structures still stand, several buildings have since succumbed to the expansion of Kellogg Avenue.

In 1937, a contest took place to design a flag for the city. The winner was Wichita artist Charles Cecil McAlister, who incorporated a Native American sun symbol into the design, fitting for a community that still considered itself part of the Southwest. The raising of the first flag took place at city hall on July 23, 1937. (Courtesy Keith Wondra and Wichita-Sedgwick County Historical Museum.)

Completed in 1932, the United States Post Office and courthouse at Market and Third Streets became the center of controversy over its murals. In 1936, local artist Felix Jones received the contract to do the murals, but those in charge of the project rejected the designs. The murals, however, soon found a new home, gracing the main lobby of the recently completed airport terminal. In subsequent decades, the murals went to other facilities, including the Wichita Art Museum, before returning to the Kansas Aviation Museum. (Below, courtesy Jay M. Price and Kansas Aviation Museum.)

In 1926, Fairmount College became the Municipal University of Wichita. This aerial shows the university in 1930 with the construction of the administration building, now Jardine Hall, in the upper center. Old Main, once Fairmount College's largest and most significant landmark, burned the year prior, with only a spot amidst the trees in the center of this image marking the building's original location.

Conceived by University of Wichita president Harold Foght as a school to help children with language difficulties, the Institute of Logopedics on Twenty-first Street became one of the institution's best-known features. In 1993, the Institute of Logopedics changed its name to Heartspring and in 1998, moved to a new campus on East Twenty-ninth Street.

A result of Wichita's eastward expansion towards College Hill, the city opened Wichita High School on East Douglas Avenue in 1924, seen above in an aerial photograph that also shows Roosevelt Junior High in the lower left. In contrast to the Collegiate Gothic architecture of Wichita High School, Wichita North High School, the product of local architect Glen H. Thomas, featured Native American as well as Art Deco designs. When Wichita North opened in 1929, Wichita High became East High. The rivalry between these two institutions developed during the decades that followed, remaining a part of Wichita life to this day.

In 1932, Wichita architect Glen H. Thomas designed the ornate Minisa Bridge over the Little Arkansas River at Thirteenth Street. The bridge complements Thomas's adjacent Wichita North High School. North High students chose the Native American word *Minisa*, which means "Red Water."

This aerial view shows the municipal swimming beach in South Riverside Park. Built in 1923 to discourage swimming in the river, the pool underwent a major expansion in 1938 by the WPA, including two children's pools at the north end. In 1969, the pool closed; the Ralph Wultz Tennis Center now stands on the site. (Courtesy Wichita Park Department.)

The idea for the Wichita Art Museum began in 1915 with a trust from the Louise Caldwell Murdock estate to purchase pieces for what became the Roland P. Murdock Collection. When the architectural plans for the Mesoamerican-inspired structure became known, the *Wichita Beacon* nicknamed the museum the "Dream Palace on the River Bank." On September 22, 1935, the Wichita Art Museum opened on 65 acres in the Riverside neighborhood.

Gerald Winrod founded his "Defenders of the Christian Faith" in the 1920s to combat "evolution in the schools and modernism in the pulpits." From this headquarters building on East Douglas Avenue, Winrod's Defenders distributed their message using a variety of media from publications to high-powered radio stations based in Mexico. By the 1930s, Winrod was a vocal critic of the New Deal and felt that the United States had more to fear from the Soviet Union than Hitler's Germany. Winrod's unsuccessful bid for US Senate in 1938 prompted progressive clergy across the state to organize against him. Among them were Msgr. Michael Farrell of St. Mary's Cathedral; Rev. Samuel West from St. James Episcopal Church; Rabbi Harry Richmond of Congregation Emanu-El; and Rev. Dr. Henry Hornung from Plymouth Congregational Church. (Above, courtesy the authors; below, courtesy *The Wichita Eagle*.)

PREACHERS DEMAND WINROD QUIT RACE

Declare He Does Not Represent Party; Manager Files Answer

The original Shadowland Dance Pavilion was located on South Broadway Street. In the early 1930s, Gage Brewer took over the club, serving as manager and director of the house band, Gage Brewer's Radio Orchestra. When the club was destroyed by fire on March 3, 1936, Gage Brewer opened the New Shadowland Dance Club, shown above, at 2459 North Hillside Avenue, in the old Swallow Airplane Factory.

On October 2, 1932, Gage Brewer, seated center, introduced the world to one of the first performances of the electric guitar at the Shadowland Dance Pavilion on South Broadway Street. Rock and roll was still decades away when this photograph was taken; Brewer played the instrument to accompany a Hawaiian-themed band.

From 1908 to 1953, the Wichita-based *Negro Star* served African Americans throughout Kansas. This page from 1939 provides a window into the community. Jackson Mortuary, the city's most prominent African American funeral home, has an advertisement in the lower center, underneath one for the Lebanese-owned Jabara Grocery Market. By now, the African American community's business district had moved out of downtown, with its hub at Ninth and Cleveland Streets. (Courtesy NewsBank Readex.)

As the threat of war loomed, the United States began a slow process of rebuilding its military force, including the construction of warships. Among them was the heavy cruiser USS *Wichita* (CA-45), seen here at her launching. She was commissioned in 1939 and, during World War II, saw service in the Pacific, taking part in campaigns at Guadalcanal, the Aleutian Islands, Leyte, and Okinawa.

With America's entry into World War II, men and women went to military service, leaving loved ones behind. In this photograph, Lt. Robert Howse of the Army Air Procurement District sits with his daughter Sherry. In one sense, this image represents thousands of stories from Wichita. In other ways, however, Howse was a GI of local prominence: his wife, Virginia, was daughter of oilman Archibald Derby.

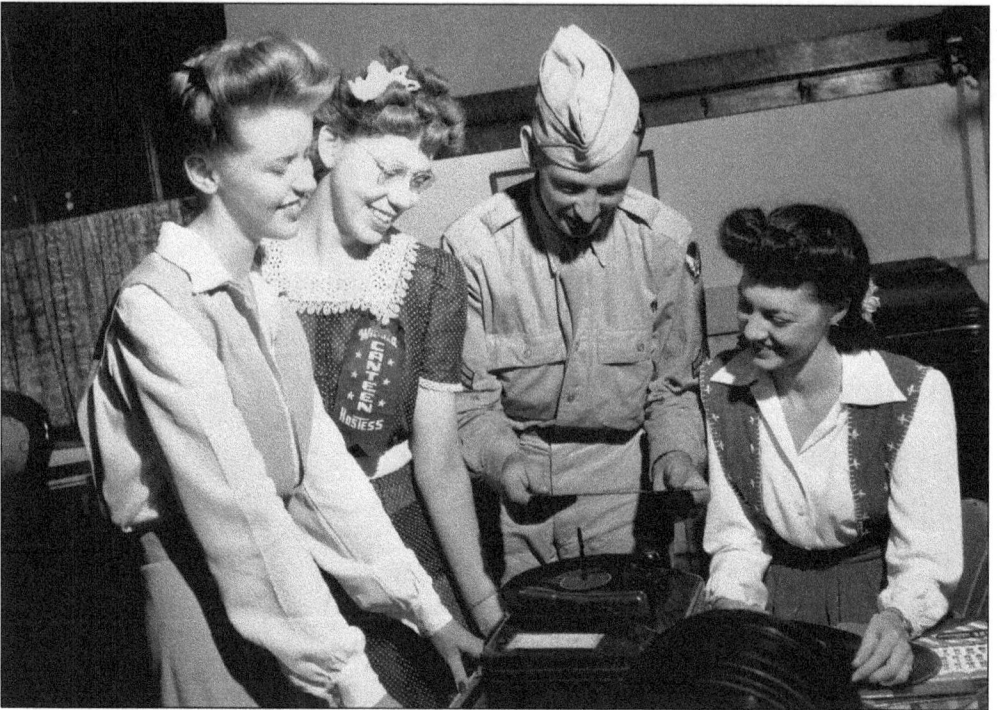

Communities across the nation geared up to help the war effort. A canteen set up in Union Station served the needs of GIs passing through. Meanwhile, rationing and shortages of everything, from housing to tires, became part of everyday life. Bond drives were also commonplace, including the one below, held at Beechcraft.

The war brought prosperity to a wide range of Wichita businesses, from scrap dealers and meatpackers to oil. Businesses boomed with an influx of aircraft and other workers. Here, the Old Mill Tasty Shop on Douglas Avenue features a bustling lunchtime crowd. Note the woman at the counter with her Rosie the Riveter–style headband. (Courtesy Old Mill Tasty Shop.)

Originally geared towards providing appliances to rural families who did not have electricity, Coleman redirected its efforts to meeting the needs of soldiers and sailors. Its best-known product was a small, portable gas stove that provided many GIs a warm C-ration meal during the war. This photograph from 1943 shows a group of Coleman employees as part of this effort.

Military aviation was the salvation of Wichita's aircraft manufacturers. Lloyd Stearman's company, for example, specialized in biplane trainers. Its best-known product, the Model 75, or Kaydet, became popular with the US military. Here, a Stearman Kaydet appears in the service of Wichita's Braley Flying School. (Courtesy Kansas Aviation Museum.)

Aircraft designs once intended for luxury or business markets found new uses in wartime. Seen here, for example, are two AT-8s in the foreground, known as Cessna Bobcats, with a Cessna T-50 to the far right. In the background, barely visible, is the landing gear of a Cadet from one of Wichita's smaller firms, Culver. (Courtesy Kansas Aviation Museum.)

J. Earl Schaefer of Boeing (center) discusses the municipal airport with airport employees, Wichita Park Board members, and local businessmen. Efforts on the part of Schaefer and other local leaders encouraged the US military to locate a number of its aviation construction projects to Wichita, arguing, in part, that the city's central location put it far away from the threat of enemy attack. As early as 1940, massive construction projects expanded greatly the facilities at local aircraft plants. Even the municipal airport joined the war effort, becoming a facility for Army Air Force units. (Both, courtesy Kansas Aviation Museum.)

Although Wichita's companies produced several types of aircraft, the B-29 heavy bomber was the city's best-known product. Boeing was the primary firm involved, although portions of the aircraft's building took place through subcontractors, including Beech, Cessna, and Culver. When the 141-foot-wide, 99-foot-long craft emerged from the plant, however, additional modification and finishing out needed to take place. One mass-modification project, dubbed the "Battle of Kansas," occurred in a few short weeks during the spring of 1944, when 150 largely finished B-29s went from Wichita to centers at Walker, Pratt, Great Bend, and Salina for final outfitting for service in the Pacific theater. (Both, courtesy Kansas Aviation Museum.)

War industry transformed Wichita overnight from a struggling community to boomtown. By 1944, sixty-three thousand workers were employed in the city's aviation plants alone, a figure not counting those working in related industries. To house these workers, the federal government constructed whole communities including Hilltop Manor, Beechwood, and Planeview. Planeview alone had accommodations for 17,000 residents. (Courtesy Kansas Aviation Museum.)

Madelyn Payne grew up in Augusta, Kansas, and in 1940, married Stanley Dunham from El Dorado. While Stanley served overseas, Madelyn worked the night shift on the B-29 assembly lines and took care of their young daughter, Stanley Ann Dunham. After the war, the family moved to Honolulu, where Stanley Ann went on to become an anthropologist and the mother of Pres. Barack Obama. (Courtesy Augusta Historical Museum.)

With round-the-clock shifts, life in wartime Wichita was busy at all hours. Here, a stream of cars leaves the plant during a nighttime shift change at Boeing. Local businesses had to adapt to this new schedule; restaurants were open all night and movie theaters operated around the clock to accommodate those who got off in the early hours of the morning. (Courtesy Kansas Aviation Museum.)

Although there was a war ongoing, some aspects of life remained unchanged. One of these was periodic flooding. Here, a boy struggles to bicycle through floodwaters at Payne and Fourteenth Street during a 1944 flood.

On October 19, 1954, Wichita's second television station and ABC affiliate, KAKE, went on the air. First operating out of a temporary structure nicknamed the "Tin Hut," the station then moved to its current home on north West Street. This photograph shows the KAKE bus in front of Union National Bank, the site of one of the country's first sit-ins. (Courtesy Joachim Walther family.)

Two

POSTWAR PROSPERITY

The years from World War II through the 1960s were ones of growth and energy for Wichita. New suburbs to the east and southeast of the downtown sprang up, while the completion of flood control projects made the development of neighborhoods on the city's west side attractive. Meanwhile, the separate communities, including Bel Aire and Park City, developed beyond the city's borders. Along with the automobile came drive-ins, shopping malls, and other features that, in time, brought about the decline of downtown. Wichita's residents enjoyed the amenities of modern society, yet honored the heritage of an earlier time that was rapidly fading into history.

During the 1950s, Wichita was a busy, bustling city with Douglas Avenue, shown here, as one of the main east-west thoroughfares. Pictured above is Washington looking west with the railroad overpass in the distance. The image at left looks east from the base of the Broadview Hotel with the tower of the Missouri Pacific station to the left and the buildings on the far right edge, now the site of A. Price Woodard Park and Century II.

With the arrival of Highway 81, Broadway Street became Wichita's leading north-south corridor, replacing Main Street. Broadway Street was a hub of entertainment and commerce with the Orpheum and Miller theaters, the Innes and Henry's department stores and, as seen here on the right, the Allis Hotel.

In 1925, the Rigby-Gray Hotel Company bought the struggling radio station WEAH and put towers on top of the Lassen Hotel as shown at right. They also switched the call letters to KFH for "Kansas's Finest Hotel." The Lassen still stands. KFH, Wichita's oldest radio station, still broadcasts.

In the 1950s, Union National Bank constructed a 10-story office building at First and Main Streets. The federal courthouse is in the background. The courthouse for Sedgwick County is on the horizon and is missing its once prominent clock tower, damaged severely in a storm a few years earlier.

In March 1953, the Kansas Gas & Electric Company announced plans for a modern, seven-story office building on the northwest corner of First and Main Streets. The design of architects Glen H. Thomas and Arthur B. Harris, it was one of the first modern office buildings in downtown Wichita. The large ground floor windows showcased the latest appliances.

In 1922, Henry, Leo, and Isadore Levitt moved the B. Levitt and Sons retail clothing store to 420–422 East Douglas Avenue, as seen above, and renamed the store Henry's. In 1948, they moved the main store to the bustling intersection of Broadway and William Streets, where it operated until 1984.

Beginning as the firm Farha & Elkouri, F & E had, by the 1940s and 1950s, branched out from wholesale groceries to include a chain of supermarkets. The company functioned under the leadership of five Farha brothers—Bahij, William, Sam, LaBebe, and Philip—employing several generations of Wichitans, both Lebanese and non-Lebanese.

The automobile was an essential part of life in postwar Wichita, with the main dealerships extending out along East Douglas Avenue around Hydraulic. Among them was Aero Motors, seen here at night. Not all car dealerships were on Douglas, such as Yingling Chevrolet, at 300 South Topeka Street named for founder E.V. Yingling. Yingling's son E.V. "Vic" Yingling Jr. continued the business and also founded Yingling Aviation as a Cessna aircraft sales and service dealership. On the night of November 21, 1968, a fire destroyed the car dealership building, killing four firefighters including Chief Tom McGaughey. (Above, courtesy Joachim Walther family.)

As Wichita grew to the east, new shopping areas emerged outside of downtown, such as at the intersection of Oliver Street and Douglas Avenue. The firm Walter Morris & Son developed Lincoln Heights Village on the southwest corner. On the southeast corner, Henry's Department Store opened a two-story suburban branch in 1954, pictured. (Courtesy Joachim Walther family.)

In the 1950s, a group of developers transformed the Ken-Mar Airfield at Thirteenth and Oliver Streets into a new subdivision. Among the businesses that appeared were the Sky Bowl (a hangar-turned bowling alley) and Ken-Mar Shopping Center, seen in this image undergoing recent renovations. This was also the well-known location of Shakey's Pizza Parlor. (Courtesy Jay M. Price)

The image above shows the view of south Wichita. Broadway/Highway 81 crosses the Arkansas River along the multiple arches of the John Mack Bridge. The image below was taken from a B-47, showing northeast Wichita. The urban areas in the lower left are the vicinity of Wichita University. Oliver Street is the vertical boundary of the built-up area. The curving line in the lower left is the old Missouri Pacific track. In the distance, fields spread out that will one day contain the communities of Bel Aire and Park City. (Left, courtesy Kansas Aviation Museum.)

Entrepreneur Ray Hugh Garvey was active in oil and real estate but gained his greatest success in agriculture, including large-scale farming ventures in western Kansas. After World War II, his firms developed major grain storage terminals across the central United States, including this massive one in Wichita. In 1959, he died in a car accident and his widow, Olive White Garvey, took over the family business.

Wichita's main industrial area was on the city's northern edge, between Chisholm Creek to the east and the main railroad tracks and Highway 81 to the west. Twenty-first Street was one of the key arteries, along which stood the Cudahy meatpacking plant, the Wichita Stockyards, the Kamen recycling facilities, and the Derby Oil refinery. Nearby were communities of workers, including the barrios of Mexican American families who worked primarily for the railroads and packinghouses.

By the time of this photograph, Frank and Dan Carney's venture, Pizza Hut, had expanded to a national franchise. From left to right, Frank and Dan are seated with Kansas senator James Pearson and the colorful Vern Miller who served as Sedgwick County Sheriff and later, Kansas attorney general. (Courtesy Special Collections and University Archives, Wichita State University Libraries.)

Every neighborhood had its local hangouts. For men living in the area north of Twenty-first Street, that place was Sailor's Sporting Goods at 2600 North Arkansas Avenue. In this 1953 image, J.W. Baum stands in the store surrounded by groceries as well as guns that could be rented. (Courtesy Janiece Baum Dixon.)

Under pressure from the federal government, the city sold the old municipal airport on George Washington Boulevard. With the money from the sale, Wichita built a new air terminal on the city's southwest side. In the above image, Austrian pines are being transported from Linwood Nursery to be used in landscaping. This sign welcomed passengers until 1973, when the facility was renamed Mid-Continent Airport. (Above, courtesy Thane Rogers.)

From left to right, Beechcraft founder Walter Beech, flier Bill Odom, and Beechcraft executive Olive Ann Beech discuss business. In 1949, Odom gained fame for his record-breaking flights in a Beech Bonanza, one of the company's most popular personal aircraft. Later that year, Odom was killed while piloting his Mustang in an air race. In November 1950, Walter Beech died, and Olive Ann became head of the company.

Walter Beech and Dwayne Wallace, head of Cessna, proposed the construction of a wind tunnel so Wichita's aviation companies could do research. The result was this tunnel at the University of Wichita. Under the leadership of Ken Razak, director of the school of engineering, construction took two years and cost $165,000. The facility helped establish what became Wichita State University as a center of aviation research.

Following an initial slump in government contracts after World War II, the Cold War reinvigorated the need for military aircraft. Wichita's Boeing plant, for example, became a major producer of jet bombers such as the B-47. Ultimately, 1,390 B-47s came out of Wichita's Boeing facilities. This B-47 was an icon on west Kellogg Avenue for years. It now stands outside McConnell Air Force Base. (Courtesy Kansas Aviation Museum.)

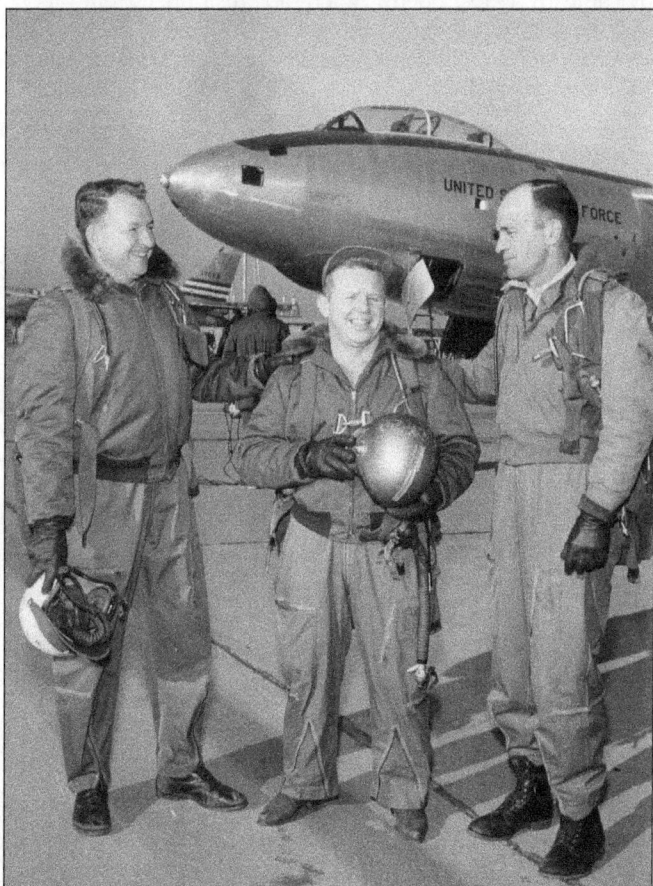

By the late 1950s, some 35,000 people worked at Boeing Wichita alone. In addition to those who designed and assembled aircraft, companies employed people to test the airplanes. One such individual was Benjamin "Bennie" Malone, center. (Courtesy Kansas Aviation Museum.)

By the early 1950s, Boeing Wichita transitioned from producing the sleek but underpowered B-47 bomber to the more massive B-52. Through the early 1960s, Wichita's Boeing facilities concentrated on military aircraft contracts, in contrast to the general aviation focus of Cessna and Beechcraft. (Both, courtesy Kansas Aviation Museum.)

During World War II, the government constructed defense housing communities, including Planeview and Hilltop Manor, near the main aircraft plants and the airport. After World War II, the US military purchased the original municipal airport to become a base for B-47 training. In 1954, the installation became McConnell Air Force Base. In the years that followed, McConnell supported a range of functions from B-1 bombers to air tankers. It was even a radar facility, as seen below. (Below, courtesy Kansas Aviation Museum.)

Originally intended to be temporary housing, Hilltop Manor and Planeview developed into neighborhoods, with residents often working in the nearby plants. Stores, schools, and churches followed, including the grocery store in Planeview, seen below. Pictured above is the community center for Hilltop. A number of these residents were transplants from the South, adding a distinctive cultural, religious, and social dynamic to the city. (Above, courtesy Wichita Park Department.)

Wartime and early postwar construction consisted often of large numbers of buildings erected as fast and as inexpensively as possible. The results of this approach are apparent in this photograph from Beechwood after a 1948 tornado. Beechwood was another of the 1940s defense housing communities.

The postwar baby boom and ample GI Bill funding resulted in a flurry of new home construction. Initially, these subdivisions were along the city's eastern edge. Among them was the home of Chinese American entrepreneur James Lew, located on Battin Street.

Kansans were proud when one of their own, Dwight D. "Ike" Eisenhower, became president in 1953. Here, a crowd gathers to greet him at the airport. Predating Ike's interstate highway system, the Kansas Turnpike Authority sought to connect Kansas's major cities through a network of toll roads. The main route connected Kansas City with Topeka and Wichita. This 1956 image shows the Kansas Turnpike Interchange as it meets up with Kellogg Avenue. By the late 1950s, Kellogg had replaced Central Avenue as the main east-west thoroughfare through the city.

Flooding had been a regular part of Wichita life for nearly a century. A wet period that saw flooding in 1944 and 1951 prompted officials to support construction of what was known officially as the Wichita-Valley Center Flood Control Project. Known locally as "The Big Ditch," the system diverted floodwaters to the west of the city. Completed in 1959, the construction took place, ironically, during an extended drought. Below, a dust storm blanketing Wichita in 1957 was part of what some called the "Little Dust Bowl." (Above, courtesy Wichita Park Department.)

KINGS-X jiffy Cafe

MAPLE at SYCAMORE, WICHITA, KANSAS

Designed for Fast "Walk-in" or "Drive-through" Service

"Jimmy" King began as a fry cook for Wichita-founded White Castle Hamburgers. When White Castle moved to Ohio in 1938, King stayed and founded Kings-X. By the 1950s, Kings-X operated a chain of restaurants in Wichita, including this drive-in on the West Side. Today, Kings-X still operates a number of restaurants. (Courtesy Grant Hewitt and Kings-X.)

In 1958, Jay Conover opened a motel and restaurant called Town and Country at 4702 West Kellogg Avenue. This was when Wichita ended at West Street; the location was truly a mixture of town and country, surrounded by fields. Today, the motel is gone, and the area is now surrounded by shopping malls, but the restaurant continues to serve "meat and potatoes" diner fare. (Courtesy Town and Country.)

During the 1950s and 1960s, the city saw the first wave of suburban development west of the Arkansas River. Indian Hills, seen above in 1975, and Benjamin Hills were among the first of these new west side additions. In 1956, Norman Bekemeyer, Howard Murray, and Jess Shade created Westlink Village on what was then the city's western edge. One of Westlink's best-known features was the Westlink Golf Course that became private in 1948 and was renamed Rolling Hills Country Club.

Suburban residents needed a host of services, from shops and schools to places of worship. Sometimes, however, the needs emerged before buildings could be erected to address them. Here, the congregation of St. Margaret Mary holds mass in a converted garage at 2448 South Washington Street. (Courtesy Mark Shock.)

In the 1940s, architect Uel Ramey relocated from Winfield to Wichita, where he designed structures across the city. One of Ramey's best-known works was the church for Holy Cross Lutheran, the congregation that he attended. His use of parabolic arches was modern and unusual for the time, the design attracting national and even worldwide attention.

In June 1950, the Diocese of Wichita purchased a six-acre plot at Kellogg Avenue and Woodlawn Street for what became the Church of the Magdalen. The church building, dating from 1968, was originally nicknamed "St. Roll-O-Rena," due to the parish's temporary home in a skating rink, but was best known as the "Holy Hamburger," for its unique appearance. (Courtesy Catholic Diocese of Wichita.)

In 1962, Hebrew Congregation moved out of its older shul at Kansas and English Streets into a new synagogue located on Woodlawn Street. Here, the congregation's leaders, carrying the Torah scrolls, head a procession as part of the dedication ceremonies. (Courtesy Hebrew Congregation.)

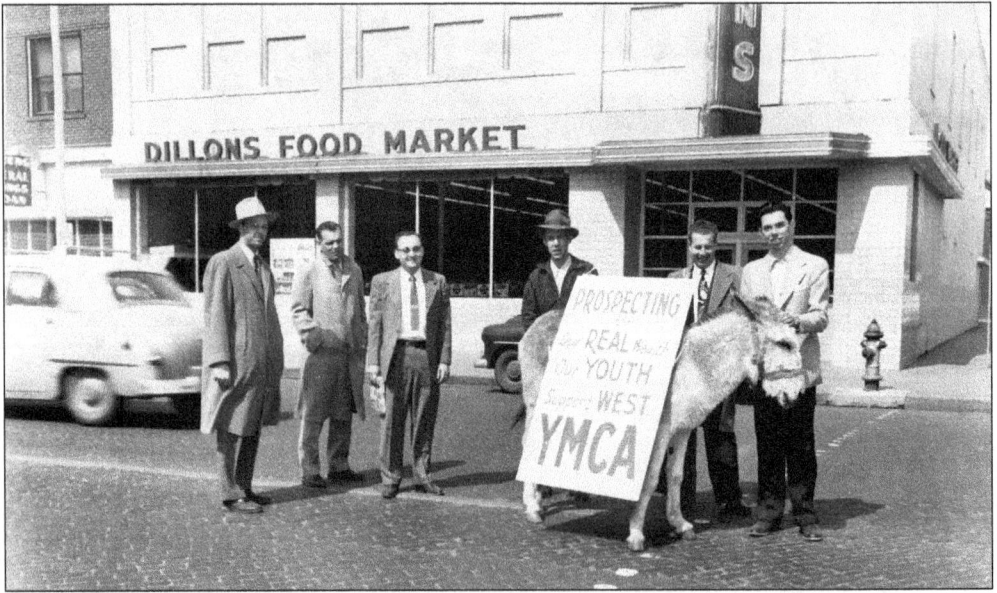

Wichita's YMCA heritage dates back to 1885, and included the support of philanthropists such as A.A. Hyde. Originally intended to provide moral and spiritual resources, the "Y" had, by the 1950s, expanded to provide recreation and other social activities. This donkey in front of the west side Dillons is helping to raise money for a YMCA west branch.

Originally called the Wichita Ministerial Alliance, the Wichita Council of Churches, had, after World War II, expanded to include Catholic, Orthodox, and Jewish partners. Its work included both international and local ecumenical causes, such as this postwar relief effort. Today, what is now called Interfaith Ministries harnesses the energies of several religious traditions to address social justice needs in the community. (Courtesy Interfaith Ministries.)

Two murals graced the auditorium walls of the Crest Theater at 4825 East Douglas Avenue. This one on the left wall depicted Wichita as a modern industrial city. Opening in 1950, the Crest Theater was the crown jewel of O.F. Sullivan's Independent Theaters. With the rise of multiplexes like Cinemas West and Cinemas East, the theater closed in 1989 and was demolished in 1997.

Mexican Americans blended customs from both Latin American and Anglo American cultures. Many families still ate traditional Mexican foods, while women served as healers or *curanderas*. They also, however, participated in activities common to larger American culture, such as sports. A Mexican American basketball tournament, for example, had been a major social event since the 1940s.

19th Annual

Mexican-American Basketball
TOURNAMENT
QUEEN CANDIDATES

MISS SANDRA ARMENDARIZ   MISS MELODY FLORES   MISS CARMEN LOPEZ

TOURNAMENT CORONATION DANCE

Main Ballroom - Broadview Hotel

Saturday, March 27, 1965, 9:00 p.m. to 1:00 a.m.

Sponsored by
MEXICAN-AMERICAN BASKETBALL TEAM

In 1887, the Sisters of the Blessed Virgin Mary established Mount Carmel Academy on West Douglas Avenue. In 1961, a new Mount Carmel Academy was built on East Central Avenue near the Vickers Estate. In 1971, the all-boys Chaplain Kapaun Memorial High School and the all-girls Mount Carmel Academy merged to form Kapaun Mount Carmel Catholic High School.

In 1956, the Jesuits built Chaplain Kapaun Memorial High School on North Woodlawn Street, named in honor of Fr. Emil Kapaun who was killed in the Korean Conflict. Father Kapaun has recently attracted attention as a possible candidate for sainthood.

In 1966, the Catholic Diocese of Wichita opened Madonna High School for girls. Five years later, financial difficulties forced the diocese to sell the building to Wichita Public Schools. Renamed Wilbur Junior High School, this building is the only Wichita school to serve both the parochial and public school systems. (Courtesy McCormick School Museum.)

In 1964, what was then Notre Dame High School moved to Central Avenue and Woodchuck Street, eventually renamed Bishop Carroll High School. It remained a Catholic boys' high school until 1971 when it became coeducational. (Courtesy Catholic Diocese of Wichita.)

Wichita West High School opened in 1953 as the first high school west of the Arkansas River. Architects Glen H. Thomas and Arthur B. Harris designed this school; theirs was a striking departure from Thomas's North High design but a model for the Wichita South and Southeast High Schools. (Courtesy McCormick School Museum.)

Residents in far north Wichita, Park City, and Bel Aire organized Heights Rural High School in 1959 with the facility opening in 1961. The school's rural designation suggested that these families considered themselves country, rather than suburban dwellers. Two years later, Heights Rural High School entered into the Wichita public school system. (Courtesy McCormick School Museum.)

During the 1950s, the Wichita public school system greatly expanded to 32 elementary schools, 8 junior high schools, and three senior high schools including Southeast High School, "the Golden Buffaloes." (Courtesy McCormick School Museum.)

Planeview originally had its own high school whose mascot was the Gremlin, seen here. By 1959, however, Wichita South became the main high school for Wichita's south side and initially embraced a "Dixie" theme that included the display of the Confederate flag. To reduce racial tensions, the student body changed its mascot from the "Colonels" to the "Titans" in 1970.

Corbin Education Center, on the campus of Wichita State University, was dedicated in 1964 and named after Pres. Harry Corbin, who led the University of Wichita into the Kansas Board of Regents system. One of the last designs of architect Frank Lloyd Wright, the facility's plan and appearance derived from Wright's unexecuted design for the telegraph and post building in Baghdad, Iraq.

Another of Corbin's efforts was the construction of a new student union building, the design of architect Uel Ramey. Corbin's biggest accomplishment, however, was the struggle to have the institution join the state university system. The University of Kansas and Kansas State University resisted, but persistence paid off. On July 1, 1964, the University of Wichita became officially Wichita State University. (Courtesy Joachim Walther family.)

A landmark of west Wichita, what is now the Davis Administration Building was originally erected to house the short-lived Garfield University but has been the heart of Friends University since that institution's founding in 1898. Of the flat-roofed modern buildings nearby, only Sumpter Hall, located to the left of Davis in this image, remains.

Under the guidance of the Sisters of the Adorers of the Blood of Christ and the Catholic Diocese of Wichita, Sacred Heart College, at the top of this image, transitioned in the 1950s from a two-year to a four-year college. In 1965, it became a coeducational institution and renamed Kansas Newman College in 1973. It became Newman University in 1998.

The 1940s and 1950s were the heyday of nightclubs in Wichita such as the Shadowlands and the Plamor. Offering dancing, food, live entertainment, and alcohol (not always legally) these venues were popular with locals, especially when national acts such as Benny Goodman and Tommy Dorsey came to town. The most famous of these clubs was the Blue Moon, located at 3401 South Oliver Street, just west of the original airport. It was a mainstay of the entertainment scene until it burned down mysteriously in 1960.

Gene Autry made nine appearances in Wichita, including this one. Here, he is playing with KFH's Ark Valley Boys. The Ark Valley Boys were a Southwestern-style band that had been affiliated with KFH radio since 1939.

Lonnie Hephner started making and repairing radio sets while in junior high school and eventually did so well that the city made him obtain a business license. In the early 1950s, he shifted his focus from radio to the new medium of television, back when there were only Oklahoma City stations. Initially, Hephner's mainly repaired televisions, although today, the firm also sells equipment. (Courtesy Hephner family.)

KTVH, Kansas's first television station, began broadcasting on January 1, 1953, from Hutchinson, Kansas. In 1956, the station moved to its current location on East Thirty-seventh Street North in Wichita. The call letters were later changed to KWCH, the station serving as Wichita's CBS affiliate.

KARD went on the air on September 8, 1955, and through the years, featured children's programs like *Major Astro*. On May 1, 1956, it broadcasted the first color program in Kansas. In the 1960s, several Kansas stations formed the Kansas State Network with KARD as the flagship station. On August 16, 1982, KARD, Wichita's NBC affiliate, became KSNW.

In the early days of television, stations produced some of their own shows, including children's programming. Wichita children watched *Romper Room* on KAKE-TV. Francis Lee, "Miss Fran," seen here, began as an elementary school teacher and made an effort to feature children from diverse backgrounds in her show. In later years, Lee moved to Topeka, where she became active in Democratic political circles.

Along with Romper Room, KAKE produced *Santa's Workshop* starring local television personality Henry Harvey as Santa Claus. Every day from Thanksgiving to Christmas Eve, Santa and his faithful assistant "KAKEMAN" counted down the days until Christmas. In 1976, "Santa's Workshop" moved to rival KWCH, and "KAKEMAN" became "Toyboy." The show ended in 1986, and Henry Harvey passed away in 1993. (Courtesy Mike Harvey.)

When it started broadcasting in 1949, KMUW was affiliated with Wichita University's speech department, with students and faculty operating the station. The first 10-watt noncommercial radio station in the United States, it grew in both transmitting power and content in the years that followed, becoming a National Public Radio affiliate in 1971. (Courtesy KMUW.)

The University of Wichita also played an important role in developing local theater, particularly in the figure of Mary Jane Teall, who taught drama at the university from 1946 through 1986. In 1946, she, along with Martin and Mary Umansky, helped found the Wichita Community Theater, where Teall served as artistic director for decades. The main performance space at Century II is named in her honor. (Courtesy Wichita Community Theater.)

Downtown was the heart of the city's commercial life, with most major stores, theaters, and businesses on or near Douglas Avenue. In the 1950s, businesses often stayed open later on Thursday and Saturday with bright neon signs keeping things lit.

Once automobiles became common, a well-established tradition of Wichita youth was to drive along Douglas Avenue from the river to Hillside Avenue. "Dragging Douglas" was especially popular after high school football games, each car's occupants proclaiming their school ties with a distinctive pattern of horn honks.

Segregation was a way of life in postwar Wichita. In response, Ron Walters and Carol Parks organized local African American youth to conduct a sit-in at the segregated lunch counter of Wichita's downtown Dockum Drug Store during the summer of 1958. By August, the effort pressured the store (and later, the entire chain) to desegregate, becoming the first major sit-in of the civil rights movement.

Chester Lewis is seen here with his mother, Edna Anderson. Lewis grew up in Hutchinson and attended the University of Kansas. He moved to Wichita in 1953, where he became one of the city's premier African American attorneys. He challenged segregation at Wesley Hospital, at Wichita's municipal pool, in housing, and in public schools, becoming one of the most vocal leaders in the local civil rights movement.

BUILD A BETTER TOWN
WITH
Jo BROWN
ON OUR
For: SCHOOL BOARD

- Creating equitable opportunities for each child in school; inequalities breed unrest, thwart initiative, demoralize our community.
- Encouraging more active participation of parent groups in our school programs and problems.
- Securing the best teachers and making their economic climate more acceptable; perpetuating competence and dignity among our educators and children.
- Developing and supporting innovative teaching methods and expanding counseling services.
- Promoting relevant avenues for accountability among students-teachers-parents, Board of Education and the Administration.

SHE IS A MOTHER ... CONCERNED ABOUT OUR CHILDREN .... OUR SCHOOLS ... OUR COMMUNITY

Wichita's solution to school segregation was to implement a cross-bussing system in 1969. African American students would be bussed out of their neighborhoods while white students, based on a birthday lottery system, were bussed into northeast Wichita. This policy was met with several protests by white and African American parents. Amid the controversy, Jo Brown became the first African American elected to the Wichita school board.

By the 1960s, Wichita's African American community was concentrated in the city's northeastern neighborhoods. One such neighborhood, at Twentieth and Piatt Streets, was transformed forever on January 16, 1965, when a KC-135 tanker from McConnell Air Force Base crashed while it was full of fuel, killing 30 people and burning several houses. A memorial, constructed in 2007, marks the event.

81

With the drive-in craze hitting Wichita, local theater mogul O.F. Sullivan opened the 54 Drive In on East Kellogg Avenue in 1947. The car headlights in the above image show the vastness of the parking lot. In addition, O.F. Sullivan owned the 81 Drive In, Crest, Palace, Crawford, Civic, Tower, and West Theaters.

Marta R. and Truman H. Slothower opened the Sunset Theater at 1407 East Harry Street in 1950. The surfing movie *The Endless Summer* had its national debut at the Sunset Theater; to prove its worth, the filmmaker believed that if it made it in Wichita it could make it anywhere. The Sunset closed in 1968 and was later home to Senseney Music.

Raymond "Hap" Dumont, sporting goods salesman and promoter, organized the National Semi-Pro Baseball Congress Kansas State Tournament in 1931. Hap Dumont later proposed that if the city built a stadium, he would bring in a national semipro tournament. The city agreed and built Lawrence Stadium, shown above. In 1935, Dumont paid $1,000 to Satchel Paige to be the headliner of the first National Baseball Congress, which is still held yearly. In the image below, the Fort Wayne Capeharts, previously the Fort Wayne G-E Club, are watching from the dugout during the 1950 National Baseball Congress tournament. In 1978, the city renamed Lawrence Stadium Lawrence-Dumont Stadium. (Both, courtesy National Baseball Congress.)

In 1949, Ottaway Amusement Company opened Joyland Amusement Park at 2801 South Hillside Avenue. In the 1960s, Joyland was sold to Stan and Margaret Nelson. The Nelsons added many of the park's memorable rides, including the Whacky Shack, the Log Jam, and the Tilt-A-Whirl. After declining attendance, the Nelsons closed the park in 2005. (Courtesy Grant Hewitt.)

When GIs liberated Orleans, France, during World War II, among them were a number of soldiers from Wichita. Thus, began a relationship between the communities that remain "Sister Cities." For this reason, a statue of Joan of Arc now stands outside the Wichita Public Library. Wichita's Chance Industries built this miniature train for Orleans.

In addition to Joyland, Kiddieland, located at 3833 East Harry Street, was another destination in the 1960s and early 1970s. Although there is still great nostalgia for these places, the days of the family-run amusement park have passed, and Wichitans now have to travel to Kansas City or Oklahoma City (or wait until the annual state fair in Hutchinson) to go on rides.

There had been a zoo in Riverside Park since the early 1900s. By the time of this photograph in 1952, the zoo was a popular local attraction, complete with bears, exotic birds, lions, and alligators. The creation of the Sedgwick County Zoo marked the end of most of the animal exhibits here, although a small collection dedicated to local wildlife remains.

As a memorial to Victor Murdock of *The Wichita Eagle,* Dick Long and other civic-minded Wichitans founded Historic Wichita, Inc., in 1950 to preserve several of the city's oldest buildings. In 1952, Historic Wichita moved the First Presbyterian Church and parsonage, the Munger House, and Wichita's first jail to a site on the banks of the Big Arkansas River, the beginning of Old Cowtown Museum. Through the years, 63 more buildings were added to the open-air museum, telling the story of Wichita from 1865 to 1880. Below, Frontierland, an amusement park located west of town on US-54, operated briefly in the 1960s. It has long since vanished but lives on in local memories that sometimes confuse it with Old Cowtown Museum. (Above, courtesy Old Cowtown Museum; below, courtesy Grant Hewitt.)

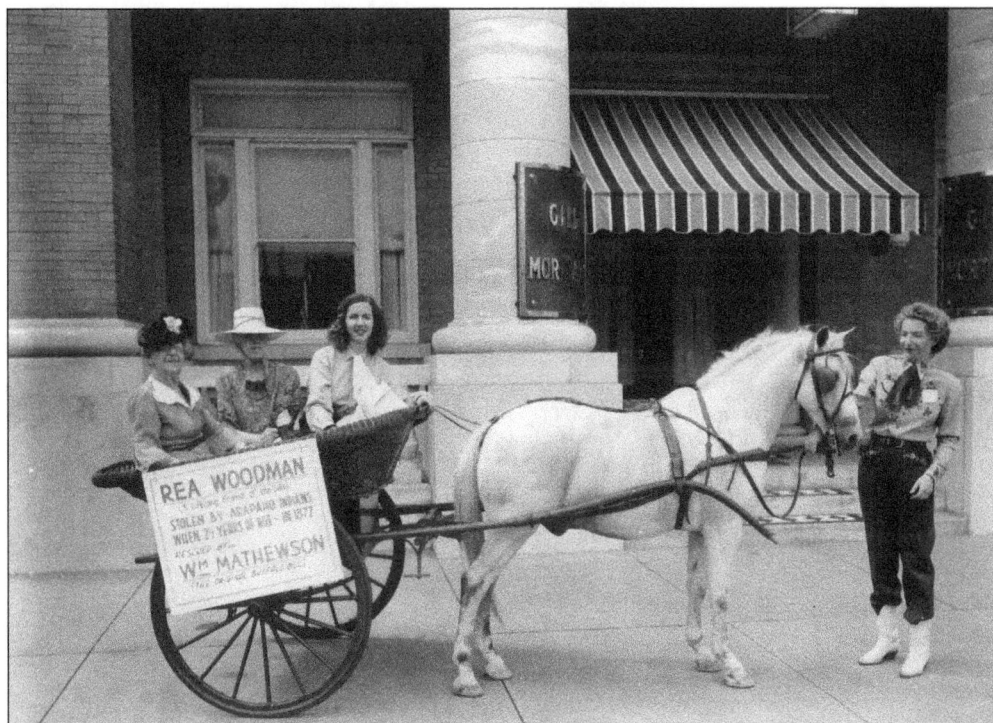

A flurry of commemorative events and expositions took place across the nation in the postwar years, as a society that was entranced with all that was new and modern also cultivated nostalgia for earlier, supposedly simpler times. In 1947, the Chisholm Trail Jubilee included a parade with Wichita Pioneer Rea Woodman riding in a wagon sponsored by Gill Mortuary. Kansas's territorial and statehood centennials were large statewide events, complete with parades, seen below, and activities such as beard-growing contests. Although Kansas statehood (in 1861) was inseparable from the issue of slavery and the Civil War, the state's memory of that event tended to embrace a more frontier or "Old West" tone.

The framework that will support Century II's great, circular roof takes shape over the spaces that will become the exhibition hall, Mary Jane Teall Theater, and concert hall. The newly completed Wichita Public Library is visible in the background.

Three

THE VORTEX OF CHANGE

As Wichita embarked on its second century, the very nature of the community was in transition. Locally owned family businesses continued to define the economy. The very buildings and facilities on the campus of Wichita State University bore witness to the most prominent of these entrepreneurs and business owners, including Levitt, Jabara, Beech, Garvey, Cessna, Marcus, Barton, Devlin, Ablah, Carney, Coleman, Kamen, Gore, and Koch. At the same time, however, global economic trends made their presence felt in Wichita as many of these companies became part of national and international corporations. Meanwhile, populations that had been marginalized or largely invisible, including African Americans, Native Americans, Latinos, and Asians, demanded a greater role in local life while family-run firms such as Cornejo & Sons or Jackson Mortuary maintained a legacy of minority-run entrepreneurship. The fabric of the city was changing as well, with urban renewal and a demand for progress resulting in the destruction of old buildings, sparking a historic preservation movement to rehabilitate the structures that remained. As the city spread outward and enveloped what had once been separate small towns, locals created events such as Riverfest as well as institutions that all could enjoy.

By 1965, the 54-year-old Forum was, according to Craig Miner, "no longer a draw, in fact it required an apology." The city utilized the help of the urban renewal funds to create a bigger auditorium and convention center. The Forum's stage, as shown at left, was one of the last remaining sections to be torn down to make way for the Century II Performing Arts and Convention Center.

To celebrate Wichita's centennial, city leaders decided a new civic and cultural center was needed. John W. Hickman, a protégé of Frank Lloyd Wright, designed the new building, with Hickman's partner, Roy Varenhorst, completing the project. Eby Construction Company, a Wichita family business, made these designs a reality. In 1968, the circular structure gained its official name, Century II, in honor of the city's 100th anniversary. (Courtesy Joachim Walther family.)

Here, crews construct what will become the Kiva Shopping Mall, with the Olive W. Garvey Building in the distance, part of what became the Garvey Center. This scene predates the completion of the 26-floor Holiday Inn, built in 1970. On August 11, 1976, nineteen-year-old Michael Soles killed three people and injured eight from the top floor of the Holiday Inn, then the tallest building in Kansas.

Taken from the Sedgwick County Courthouse, this image shows Wichita City Hall on the right with the Epic Center in the middle. Local lore says that the Epic Center's developer, having had so many problems with municipal leaders, wanted his creation to cast a shadow on city hall. Its original design was supposed to consist of two adjacent structures that mirrored each other. (Courtesy Sedgwick County, Kansas, Government.)

One of the casualties of urban development was the three-story Eagle Building, a fixture at the southwest corner of William and Market Streets since 1908. It had been home to *The Wichita Eagle* until 1961, when it moved to its present offices on East Douglas Avenue. In 1963, the Eagle Building was razed and eventually became the site of the Innes parking garage. By 1967, there was a new nine-story parking garage that connected to the Innes store and the Sutton Place office building, formerly the York Rite Temple, by walkways.

Wichita was a center for the Beat Movement's authors, poets, and writers. Charlie Plymell, famous for his "Keep on Truckin'" cartoon, as well as Michael McClure, Lee Streiff, Bruce Conner, Robert Branaman, and David Haselwood all came of age in Wichita and are sometimes called "The Wichita Group" or "The Wichita Vortex." One of the main hangouts was Moody's Skid Row Beanery, located on Douglas Avenue next to the Eaton Hotel. In 1966, Allen Ginsberg stayed in Wichita for a short time, with a reading at Wichita State University causing consternation among authorities. Ginsberg also wrote a poem dedicated to a Wichita bar called "Chances R," a club that catered to a gay and bohemian clientele. Robert Branaman created this poster of the Chances R for a local countercultural journal called the *Evergreen*. (Courtesy Robert Branaman.)

Released as part of the celebration of Wichita's centennial on July 21, 1970, the seal's "Y" represents the confluence of the Little and Big Arkansas Rivers in the heart of the city. The bottom left triangle represents the city's past while the bottom right triangle represents Wichita's oil, aviation, and agricultural businesses. The top triangle features Century II, now the city's most recognizable landmark. (Courtesy the authors.)

In 1970, Wichita celebrated its rivers with the Wichitennial Water Festival, renamed the Wichitennial River Festival, in 1972. In later years, it became the Wichita River Festival and featured block parties, ice cream socials, musical entertainment, fireworks, and bathtub races on the river as shown above.

In 1969, a group of businessmen commissioned artist James Rosati to create a sculpture in honor of Wichita's centennial. During his first visit to the city, Rosati said, "The Wichita horizon is exciting. I want to honor your space." Not every Wichitan felt honored by the *Wichita Tripodal*, dedicated on March 8, 1972, however. The sculpture and its message remains a source of controversy to this day.

As part of the celebration of the American bicentennial, representatives of Kansas Gas & Electric Company and various city employees hired Kiowa-Comanche artist Blackbear Bosin to design the 44-foot-tall *Keeper of the Plains*. Here, Bosin, on the right, explains models of his iconic sculpture with local officials. Dedicated on May 16, 1974, the sculpture soon became the main symbol for Wichita and Sedgwick County.

When Calvary Baptist Church moved to its new home, which was the work of African American architect Charles McAfee, urban renewal threatened the old building with demolition. Several figures, including Doris Kerr Larkins, established what has become The Kansas African American Museum to give the old church a new purpose. The location, however, has changed dramatically, surrounded by the Sedgwick County Jail. (Courtesy Sedgwick County, Kansas, Government.)

As part of Wichita's centennial celebration, several Native Americans including Blackbear Bosin and Jay Hunter met to establish a regional center for Indian culture. From this meeting came the Mid-America All-Indian Center. It opened on May 23, 1976 and is situated nearby Blackbear Bosin's iconic *Keeper of the Plains* at the confluence of the Big and Little Arkansas Rivers. (Courtesy the authors.)

In 1923, Walter L. Love along with Harry Horner formed the Horner-Love Printing and Box Company, producing its first corrugated cardboard box in 1926. Four years later, the partnership ended, and the company, renamed Love Box, remained locally owned until 2005.

Fred Koch (right) came to Wichita to get involved in the oil industry. After World War II, his firm developed into what has become Koch Industries, one of the largest privately owned companies in the United States. His sons, David (left), Charles (center), and Bill (not shown) have become entrepreneurs in their own right and increasingly known for their support of a wide range of causes and projects, both locally and nationwide. (Courtesy Koch Industries, Inc.)

Inspired by the book *Nutrition and Your Mind*, Olive White Garvey sought out Dr. Hugh Riordan, who studied the role of food and mental health. With Garvey's support, Riordan founded the Center for the Improvement of Human Functioning International, Inc., in 1975, and the facility, known as the Pyrodomes, has been a feature along North Hillside Avenue ever since. Here, Garvey speaks at the dedication. (Courtesy Riordan Clinic.)

After his passing in 1967, Beech Aviation executive John P. Gaty stipulated that his estate be used to support conservative causes, its trustees meeting in Wichita. William F. Buckley is pictured polishing the hubcap with Strom Thurmond standing next to him, and Barry Goldwater is not pictured. This gathering was one of the first meetings of the era's major conservative thinkers.

Lakeview Development Company started building the Twin Lakes Shopping Center on sand pits owned by the Ritchie brothers at Twenty-first and Amidon Streets in 1963. The shopping center opened in 1965. Two years later, two indoor theaters opened, representing a move away from the drive-ins that were so popular in the 1950s.

In 1946, Harry Shepler bought what was already a long-established harness and saddle company, renamed it Harry Shepler's Saddle and Leather Company and moved it to 452 North Main Street. Fifteen years later, the store moved to its present location at 6501 West Kellogg Drive. When the Dry family purchased the business, they kept the name Shepler, which has become known nationally for its selection of Western wear.

In 1975, Henry's announced that it would rent space in the new Towne East Square Mall at Kellogg Drive and Rock Road. Here, Leo Levitt, president of Henry's, is posing in the men's department of this new branch. In 1981, Henry's opened another branch, seen below, this time in Towne West Square near I-235 and Kellogg Avenue, although this one lasted only seven years. Meanwhile, Henry's closed its downtown store, one of several major establishments to abandon the city's core.

With Wichita's population moving eastward, once undeveloped areas, such as Rock Road, became new residential and shopping corridors. In the above image, the development of Central Avenue and Rock Road is just getting started with the removal of land for the future Piccadilly Square. The image below is an architectural drawing of the new $35-million Kellogg Mall; the name changed to Towne East Square Mall just before its opening in 1975. These new shopping venues spelled the demise of the once-bustling retail scene around Douglas Avenue and Broadway Street.

Sand along the Arkansas River in northwest Wichita is of particularly high quality, and several companies started excavating and dredging sand for use in construction and other industries. This dredging created a series of sand pits that filled with water, havens for generations of Wichita youth to swim and gather. In recent years, several have become the centers of new suburban housing developments.

In the early 1960s, the Bureau of Reclamation built a dam across the north fork of the Ninnescah River to provide a source of water for Wichita and for flood control. Completed in 1965, the dam formed Lake Cheney, which is also a regional recreation site.

When the delivery of atomic weapons shifted from bombers to missiles, the US military set up sites, including those for the Titan II intercontinental ballistic missile. McConnell Air Force Base was one of these "Strategic Missile Wings" that oversaw 18 missiles in silos around the city. This oxygen tank is part of a public relations event, clearly intended to showcase the benefits of having such defenses.

McConnell Air Force Base was home to several units that served Cold War needs. Here, families of those in the 184th Tactical Fighter Group, Kansas Air National Guard, look on as the airmen stand in formation. Although the Vietnam Conflict was at its height, the 184th saw service in Korea during 1968 and 1969 in response to North Korea's capture of the USS *Pueblo*.

Military and general aviation have been the cornerstones of the aircraft industry in Wichita, with Boeing being the largest presence until the turn of the millennium. Boeing Wichita has been responsible, for example, for the building of the KC-135 since 1969. In the above image, a KC-135 refuels Air Force One, itself maintained in Wichita. From 1983 to 2013, Boeing Wichita produced the fuselages for 737s that were eventually assembled in Renton, Washington. In 2005, Boeing Wichita's military and civilian branches split, with the civilian branch becoming part of Spirit AeroSystems. The military side continued through 2013, when its activities began to be transferred to other facilities. (Above, courtesy Kansas Aviation Museum; below, courtesy Spirit AeroSystems.)

William Lear began as a specialist in aviation electronics. By the 1950s, he ventured into building his own airplanes, specializing in small luxury aircraft for executives. He looked for a suitable location to develop this market, selecting Wichita. Lear's specialty was adapting jet engine technology for personal aircraft. With the first Learjet appearing in 1963, Wichita became one of the birthplaces of the corporate jet.

By the time of this photograph, which shows, from left to right, Velma Wallace, Dwayne Wallace, and Olive Ann Beech, the very nature of general aviation in Wichita was in flux. Wichita's most prominent female executive, Olive Ann Beech, ran Beechcraft from 1950 until Raytheon purchased the company in 1980. In 1985, General Dynamic Corporation purchased Cessna, only to sell Cessna to Textron, Inc., in 1992.

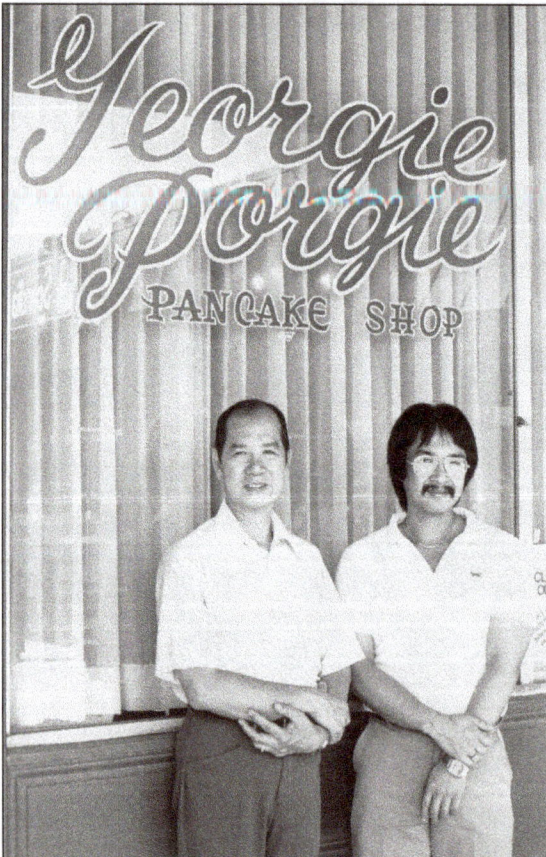

Concepcion and Rafael Lopez, both born in Mexico, came to Wichita in 1951. Rafael worked as a barber for McConnell Air Force Base. Meanwhile, Concepcion or "Connie" (center), became so well known for her cooking that she and Rafael opened a café called "Connie's" in 1963. Located on Broadway near Twenty-first Street, it has become a landmark for both the north-end Mexican American community and Wichita as a whole.

Entrepreneur Wayne Wong, seen here on the left with his son Edward, was already involved in commercial real estate, especially strip malls, when he acquired the Georgie Porgie Pancake Shop in Normandie Village in the early 1970s. The restaurant served a range of standard Midwestern fare, with one Chinese dish offered each day. It became a popular meeting place for the city's business and professional set.

The first Dairy Queen in Wichita opened in 1951 at George Washington Boulevard and Lincoln Street. The intersection was a bustling hub of business in the postwar years, with Boulevard Plaza Shopping Center at one corner and a Sears at the other. In recent years, many of those early businesses have moved or closed, but the "Little Dairy Queen" remains a neighborhood hub.

In 1951, Jack Robard opened Jack's North Hi Carryout on Thirteenth Street, right across from Wichita North High School. In 1971, longtime employee Nola Beham bought the restaurant and ran it for 32 years. Several owners later, the longtime local eatery is still going strong. (Courtesy Keith Wondra.)

On October 2, 1970, a Martin 404, carrying players, coaches and boosters of WSU's football team crashed near Silver Plume, Colorado. Of the 40 people on board, 29 died on the mountain and two later died in the hospital. On November 20, 1971, a memorial on the Wichita State University campus was dedicated to the victims of the plane crash. (Courtesy Special Collections and University Archives, Wichita State University Libraries.)

Wichita State University's Edwin A. Ulrich Museum of Art, named in honor of one of its main benefactors, opened in 1974. The museum's building was another creation of architect Charles McAfee. The Martin H. Bush outdoor sculpture garden is one of the largest on a university campus and includes Joan Miro's glass and marble mural *Personnages Oiseaux*, or "Bird People," which graces the museum's entrance. (Courtesy Keith Wondra.)

The Wichita Symphony Orchestra formed in 1944 with its first home in Wichita East High School's auditorium. According to symphony supporter Bill Sloan, there was no air conditioning, and on hot days, the windows were open. Along with hearing the music, one could also hear airplanes flying overhead. In 1969, the symphony moved to the new Century II Performing Arts and Convention Center.

In addition to Catholic schools, Wichita's private school heritage includes Wichita Collegiate. Its roots go back to a merger in 1962 of the Ethel Spaulding Nursery School and the Independent Day School. The main school building, located on East Central Avenue, dates from 1964. (Courtesy Wichita Collegiate School.)

For a number of years, the Wichita Historical Museum operated out of a converted mansion on Douglas Avenue. The museum's fortunes changed, however, with the construction of a new Wichita city hall on North Main Street. Rather than demolish the old city building, municipal leaders allowed the historical museum to inhabit the space after an extensive remodeling effort. The museum was almost ready to open its doors in its new location when, on June 22, 1981, lightning struck the tower and caused a fire. Fortunately, the damage was minor, and the institution that is now the Wichita-Sedgwick County Historical Museum has occupied the old city hall ever since. (Below, courtesy Jay M. Price.)

With the Wichita Art Museum running out of space, the museum commissioned Edward Larrabee Barnes to design an addition that surrounded the original 1935 building. In 2003, the museum expanded once again. Originally, the Wichita Art Museum and the Wichita Art Association were one organization. In 1942, the partnership ended when the art association bought the Hurd Estate in the College Hill neighborhood. Thirteen years later, it moved to its present location on East Central Avenue, shown below, and later changed its name in 1990 to the Wichita Center for the Arts.

When Century II proved unsuitable to host a circus, it became apparent that Wichita needed a livestock and agricultural exhibit hall. In 1974, the Sedgwick County Commission bought 240 acres near the town of Park City and hired Dondlinger and Sons, a longtime Wichita construction firm, to erect what became the Kansas Coliseum. (Courtesy Sedgwick County, Kansas, Government.)

By the mid-1960s, the zoo in Riverside Park seemed far too small, so the Sedgwick County Zoological Society held several parades and benefits to rally the community. In 1966, a bond issue passed, and a new zoo opened on the city's northwest side in 1971. The American Farm, shown here, along with the Asian Farm, were the first of what are now several exhibits and habitats. (Courtesy KPTS.)

After many years of effort, Botanica, The Wichita Gardens, opened on May 31, 1987. During its grand opening, Wichita mayor Bob Knight and city councilwoman Sally Dewey cut the ribbon. Beginning primarily as a garden center, it has become a community gathering space. (Courtesy Botanica, The Wichita Gardens.)

The Sunflower Educational Television Corporation began its public television broadcasting career in 1970. One of the station's early fundraising efforts involved the station's personnel staying in this trailer, elevated on a crane next to Kellogg Avenue, until a certain number of fruitcakes had been sold. In 1978, Sunflower Educational Television Corporation changed its name to the Kansas Public Television Service (KPTS). (Courtesy KPTS.)

"Gone with the Wind"
60TH ANNIVERSARY SHOWING
ORPHEUM
GONE WITH THE WIND
SATURDAY OCT. 9, 1999 — 2 P.M. & 7 P.M.
SUNDAY OCT. 10, 1999 — 2 P.M.

ADMIT ONE
$5
DONATION
ORPHEUM THEATRE
1ST & BROADWAY
WICHITA, KANSAS

On February 17, 1940, the Orpheum hosted the Kansas premiere of *Gone With the Wind*. This film caused Wichitan Hattie McDaniel to become the first African American to be nominated for (and to win) an Oscar. This ticket commemorates the Orpheum Theatre's 60th anniversary celebration of the film's release. After the Miller Theatre's demolition in 1973, seen below, the Orpheum became Wichita's remaining downtown movie palace. The Orpheum closed in 1978 and was left unused until 1995. Since then, restoration work has taken place, and the Orpheum has become one of Wichita's major entertainment venues. The inclusion of the Orpheum and the Miller Theatre promoted Broadway Street as Wichita's theater district. (Above, courtesy the Orpheum Theatre; below, courtesy *The Wichita Eagle–Beacon* and the Orpheum Theatre.)

Years after its closing in 1970, the once-proud Allis Hotel sat vacant at Broadway and William Streets. After several attempts to save the building failed, it was demolished in 1996. Although the site is now a parking lot, the demolition helped advance historic preservation in the city. (Courtesy James Crawford.)

Kellogg Avenue, seen here at Bluff Street, near where the Carneys set up their first Pizza Hut, was an important road but not the main east-west corridor through the city that it has since become. These buildings here have long since succumbed to the expansion of Kellogg. (Courtesy Thane Rogers.)

By the 1970s, portions of downtown had fallen into such disrepair that, according to the *Wichitan*, "Old Town was the rough, tough warehouse district. And also the rowdy railroad district. And also the red-light district. We're talking working men and women of ill repute, soiled doves who perched in houses that were not home." By the 1990s, however, a redevelopment of the warehouse district that became "Old Town" took place. One of the most prominent examples of this effort was the conversion of the Keen Kutter building into the luxurious "Hotel at Old Town." (Below, courtesy Keith Wondra.)

In 1971, the Kansas Board of Regents approved the creation of a Wichita branch of the University of Kansas Medical School. The facility admitted its first students in 1974. Under the guidance of Dr. D. Cramer Reed, the school first operated out of a house on East Seventeenth Street and, later, Fairmount Towers on Wichita State's campus. By 1977, the program moved into larger quarters: the former Sedgwick County hospital.

Donna Sweet attended Wichita State University on a Gore Scholarship and went on to pursue a career in immunology. While finishing her residency in 1982, Sweet began looking into what was then a newly recognized disease, AIDS. She has since devoted her career to the treatment of people with HIV/AIDS, becoming one of the nation's leading specialists on the issue. (Courtesy KU Medical Center.)

Although best known for developing Rent-A-Center with partner W. Frank Barton, Tom Devlin, like many Wichita entrepreneurs, has supported a number of ventures. These have ranged from real estate to a line of specialty motorcycles called Big Dog. Here, Devlin, on the left, celebrates his birthday with the Beach Boys. (Courtesy Myra Devlin.)

"Hatman" Jack Kellogg developed a specialty in making custom hats, with clients including celebrities and movie studios. Since 1976, his store has been one of the anchors of the business district of Delano, and Kellogg has himself been a major force behind the redevelopment of what began as Wichita's seedy neighborhood on the west side of the river. (Courtesy Jack Kellogg.)

Wichita's Asian population remained relatively small until the 1970s and 1980s, when a number of groups arrived in the wake of the Vietnam Conflict. Meanwhile, engineering programs at Wichita State University drew students from India, Pakistan, and South Asia. To meet the needs of these varied groups, the Wichita Asian Association formed in 1981. Among the association's best-known activities has been an annual Asian festival. (Courtesy Wichita Asian Association.)

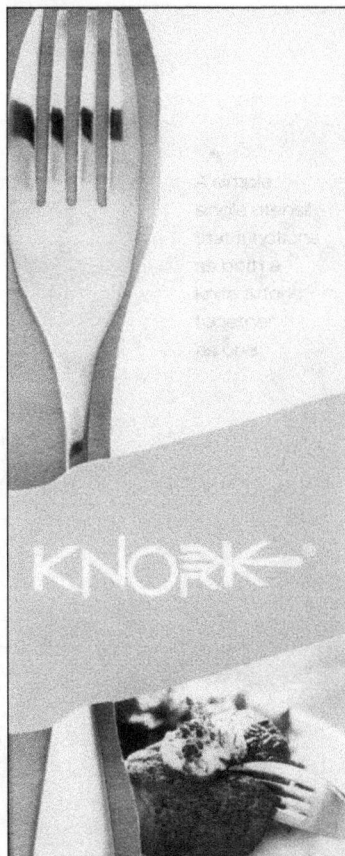

In recent years, Wichita's entrepreneurial spirit has included the efforts of Mike Miller. While attempting to eat pizza with regular utensils, he wondered about the possibility of combining the knife and fork into a single implement. The result was the "Knork," which debuted at the Kansas State Fair in 2003. The company was founded in Wichita and is now headquartered in nearby Newton. ("Kourtesy Knork.")

Fearing a layoff at Boeing, Angelo Fasciano and his wife, Ann, decided to open a pizza house at Pawnee and Laura Streets in 1960. In 1961, they moved the restaurant to Harry Street and Hillside Avenue, with spaghetti and submarine sandwiches added to the menu. The restaurant later moved to South Oliver Street, closing in 2006. (Courtesy the authors.)

On July 4, 1930, Tom McEvoy opened the first Nu Way at 1416 West Douglas Avenue. Selling a loose, crumbly hamburger with homemade onion rings and root beer, Nu Way has since grown to include several restaurants. Here, longtime employee Angel Ouellette is in the kitchen making the restaurant's crumbly mainstay. (Courtesy Nu Way.)

Since the 1960s, the city's growing northwest side needed a new high school. The school district purchased land at Thirteenth Street and Tyler Road in 1967, and, after years of study, Northwest High School opened in the fall of 1978 as Wichita's seventh and newest public high school. The school colors are blue and gold with the Grizzly Bear as its mascot. (Courtesy McCormick School Museum.)

The Garvey family's philanthropic tradition included Jean Garvey's support for a private school geared more towards middle-income families. The result was the Independent School, opening in 1980 with eight students. Here, students play outside the original school building on South Bluffview Street. In 1985, the school relocated to East Douglas Avenue and has since added a middle school and upper school curriculum. (Courtesy Karen Norton and the Independent School.)

On April 15, 1979, a crowd gathered at Herman Hill Park on the city's southwest side to attend a Ted Nugent concert. Late in the afternoon, Wichita Police officers issued tickets for illegally parked vehicles and other activities, starting a riot that ended with the arrests of 84 adults and juveniles, injuries to 27 police officers and 22 civilians, and 27 damaged police vehicles. A little over a year later, Wichita police had to deal with another riot near Twenty-first and Grove Streets on the city's northeast side. After an erroneous report that "police had thrown a black child through a store front," a growing crowd started throwing objects at police and city vehicles. One consequence was an effort to improve relationships between the police and local neighborhoods. (Above, courtesy Wichita Police Department; below, courtesy MyPictureman.)

NOW THAT OPERATION RESCUE'S LEAVING TOWN, LET'S CONSIDER SOME OF THE HAPPY CONSEQUENCES OF THE DIVISIVE SUMMER OF '91...

SHORTER CHRISTMAS CARD LISTS!

ONLY ONE BOX OF CARDS?

WELL, THE SMITHS AREN'T SPEAKING TO US ANYMORE, NEITHER ARE THE LOOPHERS, NOR THE KORTCHMIERS.

THE KELLOGG EXPANSION PROJECT IS NO LONGER NECESSARY!

WHERE'S ALL THE CARS?

EVERYBODY GOT IN THE HABIT OF DRIVING AROUND KELLOGG TO AVOID THE PROTESTERS

POLITICAL ADS FOR EVERY FUTURE ELECTION WILL BE NICE AND SHORT!

VOTE FOR ME. PETE DUMWHIFFLE, FOR COUNTY SALAD BAR INSPECTOR. I'M PRO-LIFE!

AND BEST OF ALL, WE CAN REPLACE OUR 'WIZARD OF OZ' IMAGE WITH A NEW ONE!

WHERE'S ALL THE DOROTHY AND SCARECROW FIGURINES?

KANSAS SOUVENIRS

WE'VE REPLACED 'EM WITH THESE LITTLE WIND-UP BABY-STEPPING DEMONSTRATORS!

During the summer of 1991, Wichita became the hotbed of antiabortion protests. The "Summer of Mercy" started out as a peaceful protest on the part of groups such as Operation Rescue, later resulting in clashes with police when the protesters blocked patients from entering Wichita's abortion clinics, including that of Dr. George Tiller. In addition to protesting abortion, a number of figures became politically active as well, forming the basis of an activist conservative Republican presence that reshaped local and state politics in the 1990s. In 1994, conservatives defeated Democratic representative Dan Glickman in his reelection bid for the US House of Representatives. Social issues and the ascendancy of a more free-market approach to economics enabled Republican Todd Tiahrt to be the representative of what had once been seen as a Democratic, union-oriented stronghold. (Above, courtesy *The Wichita Eagle*.)

Dan! Glickman has Kansas on his mind

The Wichita Eagle

Good Morning!
Nixon Tape Erased,
Experts Conclude, 3A.

WICHITA, KANSAS 67201, WEDNESDAY, JANUARY 16, 1974

Price 10 Cents

Four in Wichita Family Found Brutally Slain

Another Picture, 6A.
Four members of a family were found "brutally...

The victims of the mass slaying were bound, gagged and had cords around their necks. Officials said the knots...

"This borders on a type of execution," he said.
The time of death was not...

As far as the investigation had gone Tuesday night, Hannon said it appeared they were "a very good family..."

In early 1974, four members of the Otero family were found murdered at their home on Edgemoor Street. The killer, known as "BTK" for "Bind, Torture, Kill," was responsible for a total of 10 murders in the local area. His identity remained a mystery until 2005, when Park City resident Dennis Rader confessed to being BTK. (Courtesy *The Wichita Eagle*.)

Severe weather has long been part of the local story. A 1948 tornado's damage appears on page 59. In 1965, a tornado damaged homes near Woodlawn and Thirteenth Streets. In 1991, an especially destructive tornado ravaged the city's southern and southeastern flank, devastating Haysville, and, seen here, McConnell Air Force Base before hitting Andover. In 1999, Haysville received another hit. In 2012, a tornado caused extensive damage to buildings at Boeing and Spirit AeroSystems. (Courtesy 22nd Air Refueling Wing.)

From 1990 to 1993, Wichita got national attention when it hosted the Miss USA pageant from Century II. Here, Miss USA host Dick Clark is on the left, and the 1990 winner Carole Gist—the first African American to win the title—is fourth from the right. In 1991, Kelli McCarty became the first Kansan to win Miss USA. (Courtesy Wichita Park Department.)

A 1990s Wichita band, Scroat Belly, included members Kirk Rundstrom and Wayne Gottstine. Rundstrom then teamed up with Jeff Eaton and Eric Mardis to form Split Lip Rayfield, seen here at the Artichoke. Rundstrom is on the left and Eaton (center) is playing "Stitchgiver," a modified car fuel tank. Gottstine joined later, the four creating a sound that fused acoustic country music with the energy of rock. (Courtesy Lisa Rundstrom.)

Until the 1970s, the Big Arkansas was as much an industrial canal as a city attraction. Following the construction of Century II, the city rediscovered the potential of the river. By the 1990s, the next phase of the river's development took place with the decision to merge the Wichita Children's Museum with a science museum called the Omnisphere. With Velma Wallace's support, the new institution came to be called Exploration Place. The project hired architect Moshe Safdie (above) to design a dramatic building that stood on the site of former Ackerman Island. Opening in 2000, Exploration Place marked Wichita's story entering the 21st century. In 2007, the *Keeper of the Plains* was raised, and pedestrian bridges were added making the riverbank and the iconic sculpture more accessible. (Above, courtesy Sedgwick County, Kansas, Government; below, courtesy Keith Wondra.)

BIBLIOGRAPHY

Goodrum, Charles. *I'll Trade You An Elk*. New York: Funk & Wagnalls, 1967.

Farney, Dennis. *The Barnstormer and the Lady: Aviation Legends Walter and Olive Ann Beech*. Kansas City, Mo: Rockhill Books 2010.

Hamrick, Bob. *Looking Back, Moving Forward: A Story of Wichita's Old Town*. Wichita: Wichita Old Town Association, 2010.

Larsen, Steve A. *McConnell Air Force Base*. Charleston, SC: Arcadia, 2008.

Long, Richard M. *Wichita Century: A Pictorial History of Wichita, Kansas 1870–1970*. Wichita: Wichita Historical Museum Association, 1969.

Miner, Craig. *Wichita: The Magic City*. Wichita: Wichita Sedgwick County Historical Museum Association, 1988.

Mason, James E. *Wichita's Riverside Parks*. Charleston, SC: Arcadia Publishing, 2011.

Price, Harriett K.H. *From Dreams to Reality: The Birth of the Mid-America All-Indian Center and the Lives That Touched It*. Wichita: Self-published, 1981.

Rives, Bob. *Baseball in Wichita*. Charleston, SC: Arcadia Publishing, 2004.

Rowe, Frank Joseph and Craig Miner. *Borne on the South Wind: A Century of Kansas Aviation*. Wichita: Wichita Eagle and Beacon Publishing Company, 1994.

Smith-Graham, Marlene and Susan Hund-Milne. *A History of West Wichita: A Collection of Stories Which Have Appeared in the Pages of Westside Story Newspaper*. Wichita: Westside Story, 1991.

Van Meter, Sondra. *Our Common School Heritage: A History of the Wichita Public Schools*. Wichita: Board of Education of Unified School District No. 259, 1977.

Wondra, Keith. *From the Land of Andalusia to the Wheat Fields of Kansas: A History of Wichita's Historic Orpheum Theatre*. Charleston, SC: Createspace, 2011.

Yearout, Joshua L. *Wichita Jazz and Vice Between the World Wars*. Wichita: Rowfant Press, 2010.

Visit us at
arcadiapublishing.com

www.ingramcontent.com/pod-product-compliance
Lightning Source LLC
Chambersburg PA
CBHW050612110426
42813CB00008B/2531